Stuart Montgomery

Islands

BOOKS BY STUART MONTGOMERY

Circe Fulcrum Press, London: 1969

Shabby Sunshine Fulcrum Press: 1973

Stuart Montgomery

Islands

Sirens, Circe and *Calypso*

etruscan books 2005

Contents

Sirens		11
Circe		25
Calypso		65

Sirens

no breeze now
over shallow seas
my men sighting
the island of the sirens

warned them
to bind me fast
feet in the mastbox
arms tied behind

bullets of beeswax
warmed by sword and sun
filled their ears one by one

better deaf than dumbed
by sound
mine stiff with curiosity

ears stuffed with stones
bellies with wine
sailors beware of sirens
offering instant extremes

deaf to entreaty
obeying their orders
backs bent against oars
sea white with oarmarks

ears trained
to follow
individual goat bells
missing in the hills

tuned now
to their limit
to listen for sweet
strains and sounds

from the island
no man yet
has passed
and repeated

silence broken
by thunder
heart stunned

storms of hummingbirds
pound
my lungs

tongue parched
ears drum
eyes dim and darken

two voices
call
blinded nightingales

sounding intimate
one perched
on each shoulder

a clear voice
one inch from his left ear
which is slightly deaf
whispered to him

although urgent and personal
he knew her voice could be heard
by those around despite their pretending

joined by another voice
this time a little gruff
called his name but used the form
his wife used when she had had enough

come here fool
while we milk
your mind
as forfeit for music

songs to blind
steal your will
fill you with grief
make time stand still

songs to make you laugh
songs to make you cry
songs to break your heart
songs to make you die

brief but intense songs
mad ramraids of sound
beyond joy beyond pain

exquisite notes and tunes
long silent screams
stunguns in the brain

ecstatic peaks
make you turn
back again

and again
while they decline
never the same

frantic for
the sudden intense roar
the cacophony of agony
gone for ever

dancing in the minefield
for another quick
burst of peace

the suicidal thirst
for excess
the pandemonium of pain

for what will not
come back
never again

Penelope's
>	laugh
half remembered
>	made light of pain

sing fool she used to say
>	shrink
life's cruelties
>	to tunes

make madrigals
>	of agony
to dance to
>	and forget

celebrate the best
>	the way you moved
to the music
>	bury the rest

when things are bad
you can make life
better or worse
you choose

to pass by
deaf to the sirens
indelible grief

or live with their
mournful music
forever

grief and pain
are worse when
wallowing in darkness

better bend
with the oars and strain
for sunshine

Circe

At last we sighted the island
home of the goddess Circe
whose clear voice
dissolves the eyes and ears
of lost sailors and blinds
their hearts with her body

absolute silence like a ruler
leant over the prow of our black ship
and pulled her into the harbour
where we leapt out on the blinding white
beaches whiter than we knew which drew
our bodies down tired already by the blue sea
we shouted but all sounds died on our lips
and in our ears the singing of thousands
of confused cicadas in the trees was drowned
by the appalling white silence
which threw us onto the sand
to sleep for two nights and two days

on the third morning blue with cold
I crept out as the first red fingers
of dawn stretched in the sky
to explore the lie of the land
belting my sword tight I felt
my spear shaft alert in my hand

from the top of a wide view I saw
the small curl of blue smoke rising
like a warning from a thickset forest
of oak enclosing a house of smooth stone
my frown tightened as I returned to send
Eurilochus with a few of our men

clumsy feet and cracking sticks
led them to Circe's house of cut
and dressed stone this warm home
of the goddess was set in a clear
zone of the dense folder of trees

leaping gods look lions with huge
claws ignored our bristling spears
gambolled up to our feet
wolves with lolling tongues rolled
on the ground & licked our shields
welcomed these new friends into
their circus of bewitched men

while our men waited, still
as the air
        they could feel
her clear Circe voice emerge like
a moist silver weave needle tracing
song patterns lingering birds in their
swoopings leave for her fingers
to sprinkle emerald ebony & jade
dappled with malachite & blood marble
to enter her delicate never ending
fabric of gold & gossamer laughing

Polites pulled by her voice of moist
silver called them to follow him
through her shining doors opened
slowly to beckon them lips
thick with sound into the enchanting

offered them cushions & chairs covered
with skins of soft strange animals then fed
them a mixture of cheese barley black wine
& honey ground to a paste with an extract of
pungent insects so potent & sad it corroded
the spring of their strong tongues sinking
slowly & seeping into their bones to soften
their sharp heartache for their homes

as she struck them one by one
with her black stick
    bellies swelled
    neck skins bristled
    sniffed their thick
    pigstench saw their
    own & their friends
    hands clench in horror
    and tighten into pigsfeet
clattering across marble floors
she penned them to snout acorns red
berries hogsfilthy wallow together

held back by his fears, his distrust of
strange music that loosened his thighs
Eurilochus
cautious of the least pleasure in his five
senses (in particular touch) saw his men
enter the house while he waited outside
with the hours slowly trampling
his heart then turned back through
the forest to fetch Odysseus

Belted my armour on, the weight of my
bronze sword cooling my skin. Come
Eurilochus, I said let us ask or
even force her to release them

No, he cried, do not go
her voice is, he said, looser
than music to grapple with
like glue it will swallow you

left him then with the rest
of our men to guard our black ship
and pressed on through the forest
with my heart pounding alone
to the time of my feet to find
the house of dressed stone

a sparrowhawk circling
the deep blue
          slow sea
plunged accurate as a swallow
threw ice in my face and appeared
as a youth with fair hair & piercing
blue eyes suddenly Hermes god
of warnings spoke to me
                        Odysseus

Beware of the curse of her mouth
pursed like a dark song
will hog you to wallow forever
unless you obey my advice

First she will kiss your feet and caress
your tired limbs as you enter her house
seat you and feed a mixture of dangerous
musk past your teeth like a delirious
ghost in your throat she will rise to seize
and anaesthetise your heart

Quick whip your sword out but
touch her only with metal until
         her body
softer than music asks you to
                play with her
but first make her swear not
to sink her lonely teeth permanently into
or in any other way maim you
                              Odysseus

To protect me Hermes reached with ease
through the earth to uproot the black tuber
of molu, the milk white flower
which I chewed
bitter heat overpowered my face
bent close to the smell of the ground
as the God disappeared

heavy the weight in my chest
heavy my limbs my feet
bowed down they carry my arms
my genitals tight can feel
her file her nails the bite
of her teeth will meet the iron
that coats my mouth will taste
will drain the rust in my blood
will darken the rasp on her tongue
will feel the weight in my chest
will strain to beat to beat

With a low voice   Circe
with a low voice   I called to the Goddess
outside the house   I see
her open her doors   I see
the marble floors   dreading her eyes
dreading her face   I see
she led me in   I follow her feet
to sit me down   on a silver throne
I hold the arms   embossed and carved
she kissed my feet   caressed my limbs
she mixed her musk   in a cup of gold
Drink it down   I held the throne
Drink she said   in a low command
Drink it down   I drink I drink
I drowned my heart   I felt it groan
against the tide   I felt my feet
my feet are mine   touching the ground

At last she strikes at my heart
which beats faster and faster as I
suddenly draw my bare sword hard
against her left breast forced her
to fall at my knees & raise up from the floor
the black opals of her eyes & cry to me

How can a plain seaman like you
resist this pain & darkness I kissed
past your teeth to hurt and trap
your heart squeezed
tap tap in my palm

must be wily Odysseus
come back from Troy to rip up
the savage satin of the sea
Hermes warned me
                      patiently

to persuade you to ease your sword
in its sheath and let you slide into
me slowly and unwind beside me as
gradually as the sad sea in a storm
breaks quartz into soft layers of sand

Swear first on your sacred curse Circe
not to fasten your thirsty tongue or teeth
into my scrotum drawn in grimly as
the seething sea as I sink into you

Come sailor she said as she pulled my hand
could feel the warm dome of her belly
is firmly moving the sea you are
waves in the sand
outspread wings
in the wind my skin
will swell and fill
in the well in my belly
there
gently Odysseus

where she cried out

this cast iron fist in my chest
is beating my breath
look, I open my mouth
with her mouth and I lie
        with my
tongue by the side of her tongue
which rears
        blue belly swollen
        and subsides
        folded

She lies quiet in her throat song

She lies sleeping round the soft soft body
snug chuckle in her throat fucked a woman laugh
and her smell of her nose softly sway poked in her belly
the full of her eyesmile (Homer said
all this happened in the Spring)
the skin warm and smoothing under my hand
buried a hug reappeared no distance which is my side
of the touching

First loosen your shoulders in warm water
her hands moving over my limbs undoing
the tension and washing them in her bright
cauldron then burnished my dry skin
with oil which carried the sunlight within
and the clear blue perfume of eucalyptus in
the evening into the crimson cloak and tunic
that she chose for me and soft leather covered
my feet on the marble floor as she led me
at home down the hall to her silver throne carved
and inlaid in old gold as I saw before with these
intricate animals at play the leopard stretching
reaches for the neck of the bird and the lion is
frightened by the fish as I am my heart cold
as stone when she offered a huge table of food
to choose from as I wished to

Circe I cried how can I eat
with my limbs still trapped in the thought
of what happened to my men at your table
release them first if you can and then
let us feast while we feel joyful

The black stick held in her left hand pointed
briefly at me the back of my head and my ears
freezing in horror as she laughed and the appalling
noise of the herd of pigs in her huge hall ignored
me and snorted with pleasure when they saw Circe

in her hand she held a bowl
in the shape of a shell and in the middle
of the hall we could hear the sound of the sea
and from the shell she withdrew
handfuls of human hair which she laid
over their ears then rubbed them in one
by one with a brown lotion softer than her hands
working over their knuckles which she pulled on
to reshape their shoulders and wrestled delicately
with the edges of her fingers moving forever in
circles making the coarse skin melt in under her palms
and the bristles fall all over the marble floor and
the noise as she drew down their half formed faces
onto her left then right breast their voices shaking
and sobbing more & more like men while she held
them tighter and straightened their necks and
bent their backs back then lengthened their legs
to be taller and more handsome than ever

the marble hall echoed with cries
of laughter and tears my men falling weeping
all over each other arms above feeling
their faces & kissing Circe as we
ran down to beach and cover our
black ship as she said we should
stowing her strong oars each blade
wrapped with leather soaked in linseed
and dragging Eurilochus cautious
as ever back to her magic house where
she bathed and oiled and covered with rich
tunics their aching hearts and bodies caught
in the hostile shaking of the sea she said as
we ate meat roasted till it fell into our mouths
and lay bloated by her clear wine and in our ears
trickled the songs she sang as the seasons spilled
over I said as I held her hand in this last year
I have never even briefly dreamt of the sea

in my hand
a seashell
summons the sea
come down to the beach
with me said Circe

the wave slowly
carves open the air
in a clear echo
of curves caught in
the shape of her shoulder
thought in sea
green I saw her lips leaving
the sea
as another green wave grows
she slides in and is gone

caught in the water
              together
working her mouth
              over me
like the sea Circe
              and drew
me into her body
              together
we breathe the sea
              and
swim further
              the poem
is a journey
              the sea
the surface
by which we re-enter the earth

language has worn
white as wood
scoured bare by the sea
or as white as her hair is
he thought
of the lucid
surface of words
when softer
than
language
she touches it
or hard as his ear when
the sounds she sings ring in
them under the sea then
casts them up as she
casts up men when
she has finished with them

certain
sea words
of hers
seemed to be
luring him nearer
the firm curve of her ear
where he heard faintly
her sensuous sea phrases
sway and surge in her slurred
sea speech searching
ceaselessly uneasily
like fish
sea words slip
when
he reached for them

the sea surge
in her seething
urged
his sadness
to the surface
within him
in the shape
of tears
in bursting
into her
thin
blue skin
burnt her
grief into him

the rain
mingling in
her
hair
made him
hear
clearly
the mermaid
in her
murmuring
to him

and again
the murmur
of the sea
he heard
in her
ear
made him
sure
she had
shared
in his sadness

which is
as always
hers
in her
murmuring
and his
also in
his tears
mingling
him
into her

clear amber
they say in Italy
are tears of Circe but

men in the act she wept over
turned to insects and slept
arms aching in amber for more

than three thousand years
now dangle mounted in silver
as charms over their breasts or

worn by women on the
fourth or heart finger
for love and against age

the endless murmur
of seabreezes assuming
the voices of trees
sea silk speaking softly
to him like whispering
sea satin in blue cedars
mermaids they said
are human as dolphins
curving their bodies
over the blue green
once seen clearly
in air then
never forgotten

the unguarded
shore
is a graveyard
of waves

each wave wavers
        as the sea moves
relentlessly
towards the shore
a few more blows
measure the four
seasons – the rains came
and violent storms – we say
we will not remain the same
but rocks and waves break
the only backbone
is the island and the pounding
rhythm words and waves make
and their timing
as time and again the shapes
resemble the shape of an old poem
the writing itself
is part of the process of ageing

sunlight is sturdy stronger than Apollo
but on the surface of the sea
fickle as Circe watch her eyes
said Hermes how
                      musical
the ripples flickering effortless as September
distort your thoughts firm once as sunshine
now crumbling and gathering yesterdays
never said Hermes let her eyes
enter yours quietly in the twilight
close quickly and dream
of your wife's weakening hand
on your shoulder
remember the dying sun has seen
the death of many men

black boat
        rocks hopelessly
on the lapping
        blue sea
sky above
        and on the water
shadows
        waver
the dark sky
        moves at night
like water
        over his eyes
focusing them
        on one star
blue as Penelope
        and familiar
as heartbeats
        which filled
his thoughts
        with her
from sleeping
        until waking
making him
        feel so close to her
he slept well

I live she said
by the sea and
the sea
refuses no river
but the lover who leads me
slowly into my soft bed
which is she said
softer than sunshine under the sea
will find under the body he feels
another under him sometimes
seizing his heart and throat in her teeth
and sprinkling their dust over the sea
or sprawling beside her dawdling in the delta then
drawing him in greedier than green gripping the walls
of the whirlpool with the blue prow of your ship with
white hell bent sails billowing in the chill wind

sit tight amidships and let the rudder follow the
north wind driving over strangled seas & through
cloud swollen skies growing darker each hour
while you look for the low shore with poplars
and weeping willows leaning into the sea
then beach your black ship and make for
the roaring edge where the grey rivers of sorrow
and fire pour together into the grim cauldron
of Hades then call for the soul of Teresias
who has the foresight you need murmured
Homer in the half dark the eyes of a blind
poet can see after their death forever
if fed carefully with blood by another

In the thick darkness dig a cube
of earth deep as your elbow then fill
with milk honey sweet wine & clear water
Spread the surrounding soil & sprinkle barley
Promise the empty & impotent ghosts on
your return a single black ram for Teresias
and for the rest a sterile bull then take
the young ram and ewe I told you to and slit
their throats towards Erebus into the ditch
then urge your men instantly to flay
and burn their bodies to Hades the grim god

Raise your bronze sword greener in the gloom
to ward off swarms of dead thirsty for blood
is precious Odysseus and the poets I knew
said Circe were always hungry & Teresias will
need to drink deep before he can tell you where
you are going or how your journey beginning
with such high hopes in the harbour
will linger forever as odd phrases
torn hands stubborn

tongues in the mouth of
islands and your mind
companions in seas
gone many years
under a strange sail
travel footsore & weary
waves in a high wind
without salt or knowledge
over your shoulder
as an altar for Neptune
bitter seas swollen with
bodies first burn oil
a ram a bull & a boar
will each ensure as wine
purify the ground and
rich with honour

an exile full of sounds
wandering also lose all
as big as mountains
and arrive home alone
killing all suitors then
till the sand moves in
over the land & a people
of the sea call your oar
a grain beater planted
implacable god of
memories of friends
and make sacrifices
for all the gods in order
poured in circles will
lead you home safely
and many years later

Death will come then said Teresias
soft as seamist stealing
over your grey eyes peacefully
as an old friend will meet you here
soundlessly on this shore once more

Calypso

criss cross
her voice
weaving

over and under
shuttled round
the stone chamber

held his heart
pounding
in sudden hunger

while she spun
cobwebs
to stun

songs and spells
to steal
his limbs

hidden
like a jewel
in a kaleidoscope
of crystal

broken by his landing
at the boundary of my mind
which Zeus thinks is an island
he cannot reach
is afraid I will teach
Odysseus to outlive him
which he will

we remember better
one man who risks alone
the blows of battle
than casual gods who kill
in throwaway thousands

for seven years
Calypso had whispered in bed
you must choose
life or death
to live with me as a god
or strive
against the odds
to find your wife
who is
I believe
dead

stepped down to the sea alone
with his mind turning into the wind
single handed rowed his life
from the one island he loved
to the other he could not leave

each step a black pebble
on the beach
secreted over many winters
each pebble
a prayer placed in a cairn before dawn
broken again and again by waves
that buried his men
each wave
a ripple in the cruel linen of life
that shuffles stones from bay to bay
he walks awkwardly
touching each with his instep

another dawn hardens
his eyes
love comes in the end
to the stubborn man
thinking of Ithaka

careful of your wishes mister
wishes are lies
traps set yesterday
to make you lose your way

wishes repeated at sunset
release whispers at sunrise
not of what you need
but what your dead wife wanted

in the morning
as Dawn stretched
the cool coral
and crimson silk

Odysseus
reached for
his tunic and cloak
to follow Calypso

wearing her
silver veil
buckled with gold

a few rough tools she said
are enough in the hands
of a shipwrecked sailor
impatient to edge
these twenty dry trees
into the sea

shaped by the memory of love
so many bays you have rowed
your broad back
drawing the curve out of ships
that pass aching nights and days

time now to build a boat
each tree carved
to struts and beams
hull and keel curving
to particular thoughts

here the arch of her neck
as she reaches out
drawing each timber in
stretching the skin on the skeleton

wood
bone dry
burns in a funeral pyre
but on water
swollen like a coffin
fills him with foreboding

for sailing or sleeping
the backbone is the same
wood creaks under the strain
the ship a cathedral of timber
we pray in to keep the waves out

for the last time
she bathed and oiled him
for the journey
over troubled seas

begin your random
life again
wearing clothes scented
with cedar and cinnamon
and this coat woven
with care against the wind

listen she said
certain stars
surrounding Orion
keep the secret

your route is written
in pin points over darkness

hold him
to the left of your mast

the young hunter who
closed his eyes briefly
in the arms of Dawn
to be killed by jealous gods
pretending they thought her a virgin

the arrows stretch him still
stalking the utter blue

seize the rope and rudder
sailor
make straight for Ithaka

until seventeen
days later
Poseidon
hollow eyed
bronze green
and full of bile
found him

you put out the eye
of my son Cyclops
time for me to see

you swim alone
in the eye of my
handmade cyclone

again and again
    the same wave
in his memory
    grey
and green
    sweeping
out of the sky
    crashed over his ship
tossed the mast
    into the sea
tore the steering oar
    from his grasp
dragged Odysseus
    lungs bursting
under Calypso's clothes
    under the water
under the blinding wind
    under the noise
of the flapping sail
    snapping the yard arm
he felt the ropes
    he had twisted
break as he fought his way
    back amidships
the boat now
    but flotsam
in the play of the winds

the white goddess
once human
slim and invisible in her veil
took pity
on Odysseus
raised her arms in a curve
cutting the deep sea like a cormorant
rising from beneath
to break the black wave
salt white
she sits beside him to warn him

take off the coat of Calypso
and wrap yourself in my veil
which is too thin to be seen
by Poseidon but will still
keep you breathing

take off the coat of Calypso
woven with such brilliant colours
and the gold baubles she carefully gave
to drive fresh jealousies
into the eyes of your enemies

take off the coat of Calypso
things you keep
tethered around your neck
will drown you for sure
things you treasured before
will drag you down

take off the coat of Calypso
leave it among the broken timbers
love and violence are blind
let her abandoned colours
briefly confuse him
into thinking you finally drowned

drifted for days
half awake
against the seas

on the third
he heard
urgent waves
breaking

reefs
sharp as sharks
suck and spit

death bites
or bides her time
rocks littered with bones

my friend dawn
you cut your hair
on the third morning
red and gold threads
fall like lead
in a tarnished sea
bringing caskets of air down
to carry me beneath
breaking rollers

never could tell whether
the white goddess was real
or dreaming held him pining
for seven years on an island
merely to let him meet her
in the lull of a gale briefly
in the form of a bird
with her arms above
rising from an angry sea

bearing him up with her silken touch
breathing beside him and beneath him
teaching him wounded music
dolphin to human to move delicately
sealed in a veil he could not see

diving through cemeteries of seaweed
browned by time she leads him
through secret springs of sweet water
at the mouth of the river where she
unrolls his body from the intestines of the sea

fresh water unravels
the veil of the goddess
he looks up to touch
the mirror rippling under the river
breaks open to let him
tumble on to the shore
to crawl painfully
on elbows and knees
over the sand to the trees

where he lay barely alive
under a thick carpet of leaves
in the hollow of a hybrid olive
part wild and part cultivated
the roots of the tree entered his head
like Penelope in his bed thick with Ithaka
so much oil needed to soften his soul
abundant dreams barely happy
embalmed him for a further journey

© Stuart Montgomery 2005
Cover image: courtesy of Patrick Caulfield

This edition © etruscan books 2005

ISBN
Islands Cased = 1 901538 53 1
Islands Paper = 1 901538 54 x

etruscan books
28 Fowlers Court
Fore Street
Buckfastleigh
South Devonshire
ENGLAND
TQ11 OAA

etruscan@macunlimited.net
www.e-truscan.co.uk

Printed by Martin Young
at Angel Books, Tyne & Wear

typography: Robert Moore
robert.moore@zetnet.co.uk

Islands

The three long poems included in this book are all part of the same cycle. Each poem took longer to write than the adventures described. Begun in the `60s, a piece of *Circe* appeared in Poetry Chicago and the full poem was published by Fulcrum Press in 1969. An early unfinished version of *Calypso* was included in a Christmas supplement of the Poetry Book Society in 1976 and is now complete and published for the first time. *Sirens*, recently finished, makes its first appearance in this collection.

I wish to thank the Arts Council of Great Britain for a Writer's Award and to thank my wife for her patience and support over the years.

Stuart Montgomery

Twenty-six copies of *Islands* are cased and lettered A-Z by the author and contain an additional hand written poem.